D.I.34

W9-BUX-220

1/27/10

MARTIAL ARTS

MUAY THAI

by Tim O'Shei

Reading Consultant:
Barbara J. Fox
Reading Specialist
North Carolina State University

Content Consultant:
Khru David Rogers
Illinois Director, Thai Boxing Association of the United States of America
Normal, Illinois

Mankato, Minnesota

Louisburg Library
Bringing People and Information Together

Blazers is published by Capstone Press,
151 Good Counsel Drive, P.O. Box 669, Mankato, Minnesota 56002.
www.capstonepress.com

Library of Congress Cataloging-in-Publication Data
O'Shei, Tim.
   Muay Thai / by Tim O'Shei.
   p. cm. — (Blazers. Martial arts)
   Summary: "Discusses the history, techniques, ranks, and competitions of Muay
Thai" — Provided by publisher.
   Includes bibliographical references and index.
   ISBN-13: 978-1-4296-1962-2 (hardcover)
   ISBN-10: 1-4296-1962-7 (hardcover)
   1. Muay Thai — Thailand — Juvenile literature. I. Title.
GV1127.T45O84 2009
796.815 — dc22   2007052209

Essential content terms are **bold** and are defined on the spread where they first appear.

Editorial Credits
Abby Czeskleba, editor; Ted Williams, designer; Jo Miller, photo researcher;
   Sarah L. Schuette, photo shoot direction; Marcy Morin, scheduler

Photo Credits
All photography by Capstone Press/Karon Dubke except:
Alamy/Andrew Woodley, 7; Melvyn Longhurst, 5
Getty Images Inc./AFP/Don Emmert, 14
Shutterstock/John Hemmings, 9

The Capstone Press Photo Studio thanks the members of the Minnesota
Martial Arts Academy in Brooklyn Center, Minnesota, for their assistance
with photo shoots for this book.

The author thanks Emily Warne for her assistance with this book.

1 2 3 4 5 6 13 12 11 10 09 08

TABLE OF CONTENTS

CHAPTER 1
THE BEGINNING OF MUAY THAI

King Narasuen ruled Siam hundreds of years ago. He and his army attacked the crown prince of Burma in 1592. Burma and Siam were enemies.

MARTIAL ARTS FACT

Siam became Thailand in 1939.

A statue of King Narasuen still stands in Thailand.

The king and his soldiers fought the crown prince with weapons. If they dropped their weapons, the soldiers were trained to fight with their hands. This form of fighting without weapons became known as Muay Thai.

MARTIAL ARTS FACT

The king and his soldiers were trained in Krabi Krabong. Krabi Krabong is the art of using weapons. Muay Thai came from Krabi Krabong.

Today, people act out battles from King Narasuen's time.

In 1767, soldiers from Burma attacked Siam's capital of Ayutthaya. They burned much of Siam's written history. Muay Thai's early history was also lost. Today, people practice Muay Thai even though most of its history was destroyed.

Ayutthaya has been rebuilt since the Burmese soldiers attacked the city in 1767.

CHAPTER 2
PREPARING FOR THE RING

Thai boxers wear boxing shorts. They use padded boxing gloves to protect their hands.

MARTIAL ARTS FACT

Muay Thai is also called Thai boxing.

Thai boxers practice *jod*. They stand with their knees bent. Their heels don't touch the floor. They shift their body weight between both feet.

jod — the way Thai boxers stand to show they are ready to fight

Thai boxers use their elbows, fists, knees, and feet to **strike**. For this reason, Muay Thai is called the "art of eight limbs." Thai boxing is different from Western boxing. Western boxers only use their hands.

Western boxers cannot use their elbows, knees, or feet to hit each other.

strike — to hit someone

Thai boxers train hard to be fighting machines. Push-ups and sit-ups keep them strong. Thai boxers use punching bags to practice kicks and strikes.

MARTIAL ARTS FACT

In Thailand, boxers start training at age 6. Most become professional Thai boxers by the time they are 15 years old.

CHAPTER 3
MASTERING MUAY THAI

Muay Thai is most popular in Thailand. Thai boxers can have up to 150 fights in their lifetime. Most Western boxers have fewer than 50 fights in their lifetime.

Thai boxing students don't earn colored belts like karate students. Muay Thai boxers only have their fighting records to show their skill.

MUAY THAI DIAGRAM

PUNCHING BAG

PADDED BOXING GLOVES

23

CHAPTER 4
MUAY THAI COMPETITIONS

In a match, Thai boxers face off in three rounds. Each round lasts three minutes. Every Thai boxer belongs to a certain **weight class**. A referee makes sure Thai boxers follow the rules.

MARTIAL ARTS FACT

Music plays during Thai boxing matches. The music grows louder as the match continues.

weight class — a group of Thai boxers who are the same weight; boxers in the same weight class compete one-on-one against each other.

25

Thai boxers can also win by knockout. A knockout is when the fighter does not get up after 10 seconds.

Thai boxers earn points for strikes and kicks. The Thai boxer with the most points after three rounds wins the match. With each win, a Thai boxer is one step closer to becoming a champion.

MUAY THAI KICK!

GLOSSARY

defeat (di-FEET) — to beat someone in a competition

jod (JOHD) — the way Thai boxers stand to show they are ready to fight

karate (kah-RAH-tee) — a martial art using controlled kicks and punches

knockout (NOK-out) — when a Thai boxer cannot get up or is too hurt to continue the match; a referee counts to 10 before ending the match.

popular (POP-yuh-lur) — liked or enjoyed by many people

professional (pruh-FEH-shuh-nuhl) — a person who receives money for taking part in a sport or activity

referee (ref-uh-REE) — a person who makes sure athletes follow the rules of a sport

strike (STRIKE) — to hit someone

weight class (WATE KLAS) — a group of Thai boxers who are the same weight; boxers in the same weight class compete one-on-one against each other.

READ MORE

Nonnemacher, Klaus. *Kickboxing.* Martial Arts. Milwaukee: Gareth Stevens, 2005.

Sievert, Terri. *Kickboxing.* X-Sports. Mankato, Minn.: Capstone Press, 2005.

Streissguth, Thomas. *Kickboxing.* Torque: Action Sports. Minneapolis: Bellwether Media, 2008.

INTERNET SITES

FactHound offers a safe, fun way to find Internet sites related to this book. All of the sites on FactHound have been researched by our staff.

Here's how:
1. Visit *www.facthound.com*
2. Choose your grade level.
3. Type in this book ID **1429619627** for age-appropriate sites. You may also browse subjects by clicking on letters, or by clicking on pictures and words.
4. Click on the **Fetch It** button.

FactHound will fetch the best sites for you!

INDEX